CW01574510

About the Author

After qualifying from Sheffield University Medical School in 1952, he held hospital posts in Paediatrics and Orthopaedics. A brief spell of service in the Royal Army Medical Corps was followed by general practice in Coventry.

As a single handed G.P. for twenty five years, he used hypnosis for a wide variety of problems. He was also in charge of a school for emotionally disturbed children during this time, developing innovatory techniques in group hypnosis settings.

Since 1971 he has lectured for the British Society of Medical and Dental Hypnosis. In 1976 the Swedish Society for Experimental and Clinical Hypnosis invited him to demonstrate his techniques with children. Ever since, his workshops and lectures have formed part of their three-year training programme in hypnosis for psychiatrists and psychologists.

In 1981 the B.B.C. invited him to take part in their television documentary "Hypnosis and Healing" and again in 1984 in "Alternative Medicine".

In June 1982 he completed 350 hours training in short-term Psychoanalytic psychotherapy under the personal supervision of Prof. Lewis Wolberg M.D. and Prof. Arlene Wolberg Ph. D. of the Postgraduate Centre for Mental Health, University of New York. Since then he has been in full-time private practice in psychotherapy.

He was co-chairperson with Gordon Ambrose, Gail Gardner and Karen Olness in the Paediatric workshop at the 9th International Congress in Hypnosis and Psychosomatic Medicine held in Glasgow in 1983, and was workshop chairperson at the 2nd, 3rd, and the 6th European congresses in subsequent years.

In 1986 he was invited to be the keynote speaker on hypnosis at the Canada West Medical Congress, and in the same year he obtained a Master Practitioner's Certificate in Neurolinguistic Programming (NLP). Since then he has been conducting NLP seminars in Scandinavia and the U.K. with particular emphasis on its application in psychotherapy and education.

He has published several articles on hypnosis, its neurological aspects and clinical applications; and NLP. In 1988 he evolved a new model of Personality Disorder – Traumatic Separation Theory and has been teaching its application in short-term dynamic psychotherapy, in Sweden, Denmark and South Africa.

On 23 September 1994 in Gotenburg Sweden, he was awarded The Annie Fasth Foundation Prize for his development of Traumatic Separation Theory and researching its clinical applications.

He is a member of the British Society of Experimental and Clinical Hypnosis; and has been awarded honorary memberships of the Swedish Society of Experimental and Clinical Hypnosis, and the Danish Society of Medical Hypnosis in recognition of his teaching. And the South African Society of Clinical Hypnosis has presented him with their Certificate of Tribute.

Don W. Ebrahim

A Brief Psychotherapy for Personality Disorder

Austin Macauley
Publishers Ltd.

Copyright © Don W. Ebrahim (2015)

The right of Don W. Ebrahim to be identified as author of this work has been asserted by him in accordance with section 77 and 78 of the Copyright, Designs and Patents Act 1988.

All rights reserved. No part of this publication may be reproduced, stored in a retrieval system, or transmitted in any form or by any means, electronic, mechanical, photocopying, recording, or otherwise, without the prior permission of the publishers.

Any person who commits any unauthorized act in relation to this publication may be liable to criminal prosecution and civil claims for damages.

A CIP catalogue record for this title is available from the British Library.

ISBN 9781784557119 (Paperback)
ISBN 9781784557133 (Hardback)

www.austinmacauley.com

First Published (2015)
Austin Macauley Publishers Ltd.
25 Canada Square
Canary Wharf
London
E14 5LQ

Printed and bound in Great Britain

the general criteria for a Personality Disorder, but the individual is considered to have a Personality Disorder that is not included in the Classification (e.g., passive-aggressive personality disorder).

Traumatic separation theory and personality disorder

Abstract

Problem: - Traditional psychodynamic concepts impede intelligible interpretations of Personality Disorder (PD). Combining traditional with contemporary behavioural biological cognitive and humanistic concepts clarifies explanations, facilitating psychotherapy.

Method: - Collecting data, making assumptions and synthesising ideas. From clinical observations: - "pairing" birth and childhood with trauma, pairs subsequent maturational and adaptational separations with PD. From neonatal developmental studies:- classical and operant conditioning exist at birth. From trauma theory:- neuroendocrinological responses to perinatal trauma exaggerate fear anger and rejection, activated at birth. As terror hate and abandonment, they provoke defences of hyperarousal and intense attachment; and reinforced through operant conditioning by maternal love, they evolve intolerable masochisms. Masochisms provoke repression, conflict with reason and relationships, and underpin the ten DSM IV diagnostic categories of PD.

Result: - Pairing birth with trauma, pairs it with a psychopathology evolving PD. Subsequent maturational and adaptational separations will therefore be paired with PD as a conditioned reflex response of irrational intolerable masochisms, frustrating basic needs to separate mature and adapt; which explains PD, and synthesises Traumatic Separation Theory. Adequate insights, with non-regressive hypnosis as a vehicle for reframing masochisms and integrating conflicts, desensitise hyperarousal and reconstruct personality. Tolerating separations and rejections and trusting attachments become the outcome.

Conclusion: - Combining traditional with contemporary concepts facilitates psychotherapy for PD.

Traumatic separation theory and personality disorder

Introduction

The leopard can never change its spots. And Personality Disorder (PD) is "an enduring pattern", Gunderson (1994). Nevertheless there is a consensus for treating PD which combines advances in Neurobiology, Psychopharmacology and Psychosocial theory with psychodynamic concepts that remain traditional, Sperry (1995). But the nuclear family is no longer a constant. And PD's frequently overlap and coexist with neurosis, Tyrer et al (1993), impeding interpretations based on Freudian theory.

I propose combining traditional with contemporary behavioural biological cognitive and humanistic concepts. Creating a shared paradigm will more intelligibly explain and predict the categories, comorbidity and coexistent psychopathology of PD. And, evolving appropriate treatment techniques, it will facilitate a psychotherapy that will complement scientific advances synergistically or additionally, and redress the balance in the current consensus for treatment.

Method

From the standpoint of scientific method the study involves collecting data and useful information; making assumptions; synthesising ideas into a theory, with reasonable hypotheses that can be tested and replicated; evolving appropriate treatment techniques with research possibilities.

Collecting data and useful information

Data from clinical observations during many years in a single handed general practice with a high obstetric turnover, followed by a long period in mainly psychoanalytic psychotherapeutic private practice, are significant. By this I mean that although not statistically compiled in a prospective study, they are more than just an impression, which is always an unreliable form of knowledge.

Clinical observations suggest conditioning

I found that when there had been a history of traumatic separation from mother perinatally and in childhood, including rejections, then subsequent maturational and adaptational separations and rejections became paired with disordered personality patterns similar to the ten DSM IV diagnostic categories of PD, (see Preface). The degree of disorder was proportional to perinatal trauma and to the frequency and severity of childhood traumatic separations and rejections.

Conditioning exists at birth

Data from neonatal developmental studies, Wolberg (1982), citing Condon and Sander (1974) and Thomas and Chess (1980), reveal that classical and operant conditioning exist at birth; and discriminative recognition and social communication are present from the first week of life.

Making assumptions

On the basis of these data I assumed that perinatal and childhood traumatic separations from mother, and rejections, are probably paired with a psychopathology similar to that of PD, making its onset a conditioned reflex response to subsequent maturational and adaptational separations and rejections through classical conditioning. But to support this assumption I needed more data.

"Separation-emotions"

The first maturational and adaptational separation is birth; from the foetus into a neonate, from the womb into the world, and from emotional security into insecurity. Birth activates the primary emotions of fear and anger, Damasio (1995); and I assumed that emotional insecurity is felt as rejection. Fear anger and rejection can thus be regarded as separation-emotions, first activated when the cord is cut.

Perinatal trauma frustrates basic needs – assumed criteria

The separation of birth can be traumatic. In this context, I assumed that perinatal trauma includes not only severe tissue damage and pain, but also physical or psychological weaknesses pre- or postnatally in mother or child of whatever cause. These circumstances threaten survival. They threaten what I assumed to be realistic basic needs for personality development, which are to separate, mature and adapt.

Trauma exaggerates separation-emotions

As a threat I assumed that perinatal trauma would activate neuroendocrinological responses in the Hypothalamic-Pituitary-Adrenal (HPA) axis and the Sympathetic Nervous System (SNS), Yehuda (1998). I assumed that these responses would exaggerate the intensity of the separation-emotions of fear anger and rejection, producing terror hate and abandonment, proportional to the severity of perinatal trauma.

Bonding produces operant conditioning

Terror, hate and abandonment, in being paired with and "rewarded" by bonding with maternal love, become reinforced through operant conditioning. I assumed that this reinforcement conditioned by maternal love would form instinctual patterns of loving feeling terror and hate and abandonment. A feasible articulation for these prelingual feelings would be "I love feeling terror and hate and abandonment".

Masochisms

This assumption complements the Freudian concept of masochism, Stafford-Clark (1965), and the pain/pleasure principle operating outside conscious awareness. Pleasure in this context would be the feeling of being unconditionally loved, approved of, safe and happy, as associated with the ultimate intimacy of maternal love, that first formed the masochism.

Mechanisms of defence

Assuming that Freudian concepts of repression and identification that make defences, Hall (1962), correlate with neurological mechanisms of deletion and associative learning that make memories, Rose (1992); memories become neurologically correlated, repressive and identification defences. As defences, memories would defend basic developmental needs to separate mature and adapt against intolerable masochisms of loving feeling terror and hate and abandonment, when separating. This assumption complements the neural basis for the existence of the subjective self in consciousness as "a perpetually re-created neurobiological state", Damasio (1995).

Repressive defences

Repressive defences attempt to delete intolerable feelings by conflicting with them. I assumed that an intolerable feeling would realistically conflict with hate. For example the intolerable masochism of loving feeling terror when separating, would become

“I hate loving feeling terrified of separating”. I also assumed, that as hate is sympatheticomimetic it would activate responses in the SNS and would, paradoxically, aggravate rather than delete the intensity of the masochism.

A probable correlate for conflict, might be “a faulty exchange of information between left and right hemispheres”, Springer and Deutsch (1981). Observations of conflicting behaviour in split brain patients, Sperry (1965), cited by Wilson (1993); and inhibitory impulses relaying from the left hemisphere onto synapses in the right hemisphere, Restak (1979); support this view.

Identification defences

Identification defences attempt to defend basic needs by forming defensive associations identifications and symbolisations. I assumed that feeling terrified of separating when the cord is cut, would realistically identify with attempts to stay alive, producing exaggerated neurophysiological arousal; and intense attachment feelings towards mother, and associations, identifications and symbolisations of her. I assumed that intense attachment could extend to “incorporating” the emotional identity of mother and symbolisations of her; complementing the Freudian concept of introjection, Langs (1973). Identification defences of hyperarousal intense attachment and introjection (“becoming” mother and therefore the abandoner) would defend basic needs against feeling terrified of separating from her; and against feeling abandoned again.

And with identification defences of hyperarousal intense attachment and introjection being paired with and rewarded by bonding with maternal love, I assumed operant conditioning would create masochisms. Hence, "I love feeling the exaggerated arousal in my brain and in my body"; "I love feeling the need to attach intensely to my mother"; and "I love becoming the abandoner".

Aggravated in intensity through conflicting with the repressive defence of hate, the intolerable masochisms would become even more intense; "I hate loving feeling the exaggerated arousal in my brain and in my body", "I hate loving attaching intensely to my mother", and "I hate loving becoming the abandoner".

Transference

Identification defences of intense attachment feelings, and introjection (becoming the abandoner), complement Freudian concepts of positive and negative transference respectively, Stafford-Clark (1965). The mechanism of transference is assumed to operate when positive and negative feelings felt towards mother are "transferred" onto the therapist as a symbol of mother, in the therapeutic relationship.

TST explains why patients, half way through the number of sessions they expected, might manifest positive or negative transference, because from then on every session takes them nearer to the final separation from the therapist as a symbol of mother.

The correlate for identification defences might be potential neural firing patterns, Damasio (1995), protein syntheses at synaptic junctions, Rose (1992), or it might be within the "architecture of neural networks", Edelman (1992).

Result

Masochisms underpin PD

The intolerable masochisms of loving feeling terror hate and abandonment when separating, and of loving the identification defences of hyperarousal intense attachment and introjection, form clinical patterns evolving the ten DSM IV diagnostic categories of PD, their comorbidity and coexistent psychopathology.

Comorbidity

With terror for example, intolerable masochisms of:-

(a) "I love feeling terrified of separating from my mother";

(b) "I love feeling the need to attach intensely to my mother";

(c) "I love feeling the exaggerated arousal in my brain and in my body"; and

(d) "I love becoming the abandoner"; could underpin comorbidity between

(a) Avoidant; (b) Dependent; (c) Histrionic; and (d) Antisocial PD's.

Coexistent psychopathology

And evolving coexistent psychopathology:-

(a) "I love feeling terrified of separating from my mother" could create co-existing inadequacy, perfectionistic checking, a need to please, agoraphobia, and depression with abnormal sadness; and

(b) "I love feeling intense attachment to my mother" could create dependency, senseless hoarding, addictions, bulimia, agoraphobia, and positive transference; and

(c) "I love feeling the exaggerated arousal in my brain and in my body" could create impulsivity, risk taking, panic, anxiety and somatoform disorders, and

(d) "I love becoming the abandoner" could create hostility, homicidal feelings, anorexia and negative transference; the depersonalisation, and dissociation of introjection including Dissociative Identity Disorder (DID); and the inadequacy, abnormal guilt, suicidal depression, self-mutilation, "emptiness" and detachment of abandoning the self.

Generalising the model

Applying similar modelling to exaggerated separation-emotions of hate and abandonment evolves type specific patterns. For example hate could have Antisocial comorbid with Paranoid patterns, coexisting with hostility and homicidal feelings. And when internalised, it could create inadequacy, depression with abnormal guilt, self-mutilation and suicidal feelings.

Abandonment could be typified in Schizoid comorbid with Borderline patterns; coexisting, through the masochism of "I love feeling abandoned", with detachment, producing dissociation, depersonalisation, derealisation, and depression with abnormal sadness, suicidal feelings and isolation. And introjection could evolve DID's.

PD is a conditioned reflex response

I then made more plausible assumptions. Firstly, that traumatic separation at birth is paired with a psychopathology evolving PD, making PD a conditioned reflex response to subsequent maturational and adaptational separations and rejections.

Impulsivity

Secondly, I assumed that as a conditioned reflex response, the pattern of psychopathology is activated by impulsivity. And impulsivity is synonymous with being out of control, which feasibly articulated becomes "I can't stop myself"; which through masochism formation by maternal love becomes "I love feeling unable to stop myself".

Paradox of repression

Thirdly, I assumed that frustrated basic needs to separate mature and adapt would realistically provoke the repressive defence of hate, which would paradoxically aggravate the severity of PD, its comorbidity and coexistent psychopathology. Repression in effect would create "the harder I try to stop myself the more intense the feelings become".

Cognitive conflicts

Fourthly, I assumed that because adolescence brings reason and because masochisms invariably violate cultural norms, cause distress, impair function, and ruin relationships, realistic conflict would follow. Thus loving impulsivity, terror, hate, abandonment, and their defences, would evolve intolerable feelings of impulsivity, inadequacy, dependency, hostility, abnormal guilt and detachment, conflicting with reason; as well as with our instinctual genetically determined sociability, of self and species preservation.

Cognitive conflicts can therefore be formulated as:-

(a) Impulsivity versus Control,
(b) Inadequacy versus Adequacy,
(c) Dependency versus Independence,
(d) Hostility versus Sociability,
(e) Abnormal guilt versus Innocence, and
(f) Detachment versus Sociability.

Articulating conflicts

I assumed that cognitive conflicts could be feasibly articulated as:-

(a) “I love feeling unable to stop the feelings of exaggerated arousal in my brain and in my body” versus “I’m grown up now, and I can be calm and in control”.

(b) “I love feeling terrified of separating from my mother” versus “I’m grown up now and strong enough to separate”.

(c) “I love feeling intensely attached to my mother” versus “I’m grown up now, and can feel independent”.

(d) “I love hating my mother father and others” versus “I love loving my mother father and others and being loved by them”.

(e) “I love hating myself” versus “I love loving myself and being loved”.

(f) “I love feeling terrified of being abandoned”, “I love feeling abandoned”, “I love abandoning my mother father and others”, and “I love abandoning myself”, versus “I love loving my mother father and others and being loved by them”; and “I love loving myself and being loved”.

Psychodynamics

Cognitive conflicts complement the Freudian concept of “psychodynamics”, which explains emotional disturbances as resulting from intrapsychic conflicting forces or “dynamisms”, operating outside conscious awareness, Wolberg (1982).

Synthesising a theory

These data assumptions and ideas synthesise Traumatic Separation Theory (TST), which explains and predicts PD as a conditioned reflex response of impulsivity to the stimulus of a maturational or an adaptational separation or rejection, activating irrational intolerable masochisms, which in turn frustrates basic needs to separate mature and adapt.

The degree of response will be proportional to perinatal trauma and to the frequency and severity of childhood traumatic separations and rejections.

Evolving definitions

The frustration of basic needs to separate, mature and adapt creates an inability to tolerate separations and rejections and trust attachments, which defines PD. From maturity comes the ability to tolerate separations and rejections, and to trust attachments.

Discussion

Principal findings

TST combines traditional with contemporary behavioural, biological, cognitive and humanistic concepts; associates traumatic separations at birth and in childhood with the cause of PD; explains the neuroendocrinology, operant conditioning and masochism formation that underpin its DSM IV diagnostic categories, together with its comorbidity, coexistent psychopathology, cognitive conflicts, and psychodynamics; predicts PD as a conditioned reflex response of impulsivity to the stimulus of a maturational or an adaptational separation or rejection, activating irrational intolerable masochisms; identifies PD as masochistic feelings of impulsivity, inadequacy, dependency, hostility, abnormal guilt, and detachment, frustrating basic needs to separate mature and adapt; defines PD as the inability to tolerate separations and rejections and trust attachments.

Strengths and weaknesses of the study

TST combines Psychoanalytic, Behavioural, Neurobiological, Cognitive, and Humanistic ideas. Bringing together "known facts about brains and minds", it creates a shared paradigm, Edelman (1992), useful to science, Kuhn (1962), in promoting a common language and methodology, with advantages to research and progress.

An obvious weakness would be the argument that my choice of words in articulating neonatal and early childhood feelings is speculative and subjective. Although true, they do tally with symptoms of PD. Data from neonatal developmental studies that discriminative recognition and social communication exist in the first week of life with the neurology of memory formation; especially its "particular, rather specialised form of adaptation to experience", Rose (1992).

Understanding "maturational" and "adaptational" separations

Both psychophysiological and visible physical changes bridge plateaus of development. These transitions constitute maturational separations. Separating from being newborn into infancy; childhood; puberty; adolescence; adulthood; middle age; old age, are all obvious examples.

Adaptational separations are adaptive changes from one physical or emotional state to another, whether traumatic or non-traumatic. Physically adaptive changes among many could be adapting to unexpected physical illness or disability in child or mother, adoption, going to hospital, moving house, starting and or changing schools, leaving home, getting married, emigrating. Emotionally adaptive changes are typified in child abuse which is a rejection. Other examples are unexpected loss, grief, and the consequences of sibling rivalry for a mother's love, especially affecting the youngest child in a big family. I include "life events" cited by Holmes and Rahe (1967), in their Social Readjustment Rating Scale (SRRS), where adaptive changes desirable or undesirable are rated for their capacity to trigger stress. I also include "stressors" that trigger Post Traumatic Stress Disorder (PTSD), as adaptational separations. Added to which, I assume that those who had experienced perinatal and childhood separation traumas will be more prone to have stress accompanying life events and PTSD following exposure to stressors, than those who had not.

Testable hypotheses

The hypothesis that perinatal and childhood traumatic separations will be associated with the cause of PD, is testable through conducting prospective studies; instead of working backwards using "post hoc" explanations, as at present.

That maturational separations will activate PD, is partly supported by the DSM IV diagnostic criterion that adolescence and early adulthood should coincide with the onset of symptoms, but again, prospective studies are necessary. The same applies to adaptational separations which include rejections, as precipitants of PD.

To establish that the degree of PD will be proportional to the severity of perinatal and childhood separation trauma, also requires prospective studies. However, support can be found in neurobiological evidence that stress results "in a dose-dependent increase in cortisol", Yehuda (1998).

Animal studies

The hypothesis that PD is a conditioned reflex response of impulsivity activating traumatic emotional memory to the stimulus of separation, through stimulus-response learning before logic and reason at birth or in childhood, is supported by prototypical stimulus-response learning from animal studies. These reveal neurobiological changes corresponding with those in PD's, Cloninger (1998), and associated with "enhanced learning" and "consolidation of traumatic memories", Shalev and Yehuda (1998).

TST hypotheses replicated

Salk et al (1985), link perinatal trauma with adolescent suicide. Coid (1993), citing Werner and Smith (1982), associates health problems during pregnancy, perinatally and in infancy, with risks of adult PD. Jacobson and Bygdeman (1998), link trauma at birth with a proneness to violent suicide in adults; and Berelowitz and Tarnopolsky (1993), identify "a history of abuse and neglect", which are in fact adaptational separations and rejections, as the cardinal cause.

Diagnosis of PD

I acknowledge the DSM IV diagnostic categories and criteria of PD, except for age of onset and duration of symptoms, because patterns of PD can and do occur in childhood. Creating a combined diagnostic approach, I add a "dimensional perspective", Gunderson (1994), which defines PD dimensionally as an inability to tolerate separations and rejections and trust attachments.

TST identifies additional dimensional diagnostic criteria as:-

(a) having a history of perinatal or childhood traumatic separations; or significant adaptational separations like adoption, grief, parents separating or sibling rivalry; or rejections which include verbal physical and sexual abuse; and

(b) symptoms of impulsivity, inadequacy, dependency, hostility, abnormal guilt and detachment; and

(c) causing distress, impairing function and ruining relationships, through conflicting with cultural norms for sociability; and

(d) activated by a maturational or an adaptational separation or rejection; and

(e) frustrating basic needs to separate, mature and adapt.

A diagnostic link between PTSD and PD

Because I assumed earlier that a psychological stressor is synonymous with an adaptational separation from one emotional or physical state to another; then PTSD would in some cases become the prototypical conditioned reflex response of emotional trauma, to the stimulus of an adaptational separation, in someone who had had emotional trauma paired with an adaptational separation before logic and reason, that is, at birth or in childhood.

Some cases diagnosed as PTSD would therefore become synonymous with PD, and a conditioned reflex response to an adaptational separation. This deduction explains why some cases of PTSD have a variety of symptoms additional to “flash-back” memories, avoidance of reminders and hyperarousal. These additional symptoms could be feelings of impulsivity, inadequacy, dependency, hostility, abnormal guilt and detachment, causing distress, impairment of function and ruined relationships. This explanation solves "the conundrum of frequent clinical observations of personality changes" in PTSD and “the mystery of psychiatric comorbidity”, Shalev and Yehuda (1998).

Personality traits

Having difficulties as opposed to disabilities, distinguishes personality traits from disorders. I assume that traits evolve before language logic and reason, and are due to traumatic separations at birth and during childhood. By definition, therefore, traits are emotional and behavioural difficulties in tolerating separations and rejections and trusting attachments, without causing significant distress, impairment of function and ruined relationships. Evident in childhood they complement the concept of “temperament”.

Apparent normality

As part of a dimension a trait merges into a maladaptive variant or disorder, when complicated by a maturational or an adaptational separation or rejection. I assume a return to apparent normality occurs by setting boundaries to relationships, activities and interests. This compares with “avoiding reminders” as in PTSD, and “strengthening defences” as in psychoanalytic psychotherapy.

Personality types

Personality traits underpin personality types. In the context of TST there are four distinct personality types which correlate with (a) hyperarousal, (b) terror, (c) hate, and (d) abandonment. Therefore, I assume they would be the tense personality, the anxious personality, the aggressive/depressive personality, and the detached personality respectively. And as with PD, I assume there could be overlap.

Treatment of Personality Disorder

For a theory of psychotherapy to be scientific, it should have a structure evolving clinical method, Wolberg (1982). Therefore with hyperarousal as the common denominator in PD, TST evolves desensitisation as a common therapeutic theme; with motivation and the ability to communicate as sole selection criteria.

Insight

Initially TST desensitises through intelligible interpretations. Adequate explanations for “why me, why these feelings, and why now?” remove bewilderment and desensitise tension without risking regression to uncover causes.

Dream interpretation

Dream interpretation aids insight. For example, dreams of making journeys, of being away from home and dreams of the past, confirm the separation theme. Dreams involving panic, anxiety, helplessness, violence, crime, and isolation, would indicate conflicts associated with the psychodynamics of impulsivity, inadequacy, dependency, hostility, abnormal guilt and detachment.

Hypnosis and Neurolinguistic Programming (NLP)

Non-regressive ongoing hypnosis desensitises further, and serves as a vehicle for change by NLP techniques of reframing and conflict integration, Andreas and Andreas (1989).

Reframing masochisms

I assume the pain/pleasure complex of masochism formation serves as a defence against the "pain" of impulsivity, terror, hate and abandonment. And I assume "pleasure" is the ultimate intimacy of feeling unconditionally loved, approved of, safe and happy; associated with maternal love, that first formed the masochism. This concept probably explains the thrill or "buzz" that criminals associate with persistent re-offending; the absence of remorse. I, therefore, reframe masochisms by asking for more choices of defence, which have exactly the same associated "good positive intention" or pleasure, which is to feel unconditionally loved, approved of, safe and happy. I ask for choices of defence, just as powerful as the masochism itself; choices of defence serving the patient's best mental, emotional and physical health needs. Creating more choices is effected through conditioning, which is facilitated by reduced cognition in the trance; by using ideomotor signals to monitor and confirm change.

Integrating conflicts

To integrate conflicts, I ask the patient to represent with sensory based descriptions and facial imagery, the irrational feeling of, for example impulsivity. "I love feeling unable to stop the exaggerated arousal in my brain and in my body", in the palm of one hand; rational positive feelings of reality based truths and resources, underpinning control, "I can be calm and in control" are represented in the other. After identifying their individual defensive intentions and mutually helpful resources negating the need for conflict and dissimilar facial imagery I ask the patient to let the hands meet. A reconstructive change is probably correlated by neural impulses streaming across the Corpus Callosum, whenever the hands are brought together, Restak, (1979). Similarly, I integrate conflicts underpinning inadequacy, dependency, hostility, abnormal guilt, and detachment.

I reframe symptoms of coexisting psychopathology as peripheral pieces of work, peripheral to desensitising masochisms and integrating conflicts.

Outcome

The achievable outcome is the ability to tolerate separations and rejections and trust attachments.

This is measured by what the patient and significant others report, and by changes in economic and creative output. Failures invite feedback that additional issues need addressing. These could be communication problems, ongoing intrafamily and social trauma, a psychotic substrate, unresolved transference and factors that might contaminate motivation, like undisclosed hard drug addiction, losing sickness and unemployment benefit, and expecting compensation.

Termination of therapy

I generally terminate therapy with teaching a meditational type of self hypnosis and providing an ego strengthening audiotape. I give follow-up appointments which can be kept or postponed until three months have passed. And telephone enquiries afterwards provide research data.

Case Examples

(1) A nine year old only child, born by Caesarian Section, whose mother suffered post-natal depression, developed Obsessive Compulsive comorbid with Avoidant and Dependent patterns, school refusal, hostility towards his mother, and suicidal depression two weeks after his favourite teacher retired. He hoarded senselessly and included the excreta of his pet hamster.

(2) A fifteen year old male at boarding school developed comorbid Antisocial, Paranoid and Avoidant patterns, coexisting with anxiety and depression. He fired an air rifle indiscriminately at other pupils. His birth was by forceps, and he had a disabled younger brother, with evidence of sibling rivalry.

(3) While on holiday with his intended fiancé, a twenty-two year old male graduate developed Avoidant comorbid with Paranoid patterns, DID and depression with abnormal sadness. He believed he was the Son of God and a royal monarch. The youngest in a big family, he shared his parents'

bedroom for five years; suffered from childhood asthma; and felt intense hostility towards his father.

(4) A thirty one year old graduate developed comorbid Schizoid, Paranoid, Antisocial and Borderline patterns coexisting with severe anxiety after the sudden unexpected death of his father six months previously, and rejection by his girlfriend three months later. He was suicidally depressed, hostile towards his mother, had fantasies of necrophilia and dreams of cutting up women. He was the older of two children and a hospital birth in a foreign country. His sister was two years younger. There was evidence of sibling rivalry.

(5) An obese married female aged fifty six, developed comorbid Histrionic and Narcissistic patterns coexisting with bulimia when she matured into middle age. She had undergone two "shrinking" operations on her stomach. She gave a history that her mother had left her at an orphanage when she was five years old, promising to come back for her the same day; but took three years to do so!

These cases illustrate patterns of PD and DID, comorbidity and coexistent psychopathology, associated with a history of perinatal and childhood traumatic separations; together with the onset of symptoms coinciding with a maturational or an adaptational separation or rejection. Clinical patterns satisfied general DSM IV criteria, except for age of onset and duration of symptoms.

Satisfactory response to treatment was confirmed by telephone follow-ups after ten, seven, eight, six, and two years respectively.

In Summary

I have combined concepts from the major schools of psychology with neurobiology, synthesising a single theory, TST, which explains and predicts PD, with testable hypotheses that have been replicated. I have combined interpretive and NLP techniques with ongoing non-regressive hypnosis to both desensitise and serve as a vehicle for change. In sharing etiological and therapeutic paradigms, a short-term dynamic psychotherapy with an achievable measurable outcome has evolved. Its application in the management of PD should redress the balance in the current consensus for treatment, and complement scientific advances synergistically or additionally.

Future Directions of TST

Implications for clinical practice and policy

Separations should be as trauma free as possible. Thus, TST has important implications for restructuring guidelines during delivery, antenatal and postnatal care, to minimise perinatal trauma. In preventing PD, DID and mental state disorders, the anticipation, identification and early treatment of symptom patterns should have to take precedence over strict adherence to DSM IV diagnostic criteria, as a pre-condition to therapy. And when initial interventions fail, the co-existence of PD should be assumed.

Implications for research

Research possibilities involve conducting prospective studies to validate TST; using standardised criteria to identify perinatal and childhood separation traumas; using neurobiological alterations as measuring instruments for diagnosis and change; designing appropriate questionnaires to evaluate diagnosis and outcome; combining pharmacotherapy with TST psychotherapy in controlled trials; investigating a shared etiology between PD, PTSD and other mental state disorders; using standardised techniques like NLP to restrict therapeutic variables; investigating the role of religion, education, economic status, family support, and other psychosocial factors that might downplay the effects of perinatal and childhood separation traumas; assessing cost effectiveness of TST in time and resources, and cross-cultural research.

Other applications

Applying TST to improve choice in personnel selection for leadership and excellence in sport, industry, the armed services, police, educational, and other institutions becomes feasible. Its relevance to good parenting; child management and education; teenage delinquency, forensic psychology, penal reform and rehabilitation; alcoholism, drug addiction and homelessness; PD in refugees and torture victims; PTSD; "burn-out"; and the need for personal therapy for psychotherapists, invite consideration and debate.

Conclusion

In a world of increasing threat, there is an almost frantic preoccupation with promoting health and excellence for all; and innovative ideas currently focus on genetic selection, modification, and other biological interventions. Is it possible that TST could play its role in parallel, and create a more human society?

The therapeutic thrust of TST is to create more choices of defence, augmenting the protective camouflage of PD. The leopard can never change its spots; but it can still change, through more choices – of its spots.

References

Andreas C and S Andreas (1989). Heart of the Mind. Real People Press Box F, Moab Utah 84532. 72-84, 132-139

Berelowitz M. and Tarnopolsky A. (1993). Personality Disorder Reviewed, Ed. by P. Tyrer and G. Stein, Gaskell, Royal College of Psychiatrists, London, 106.

Cloninger C.R. (1998). Biology of Personality Disorders, Ed. by K.R. Silk MD, American Psychiatric Press Inc. 1400 Kay Street, N.W. Washington DC 20005, 67, 69, 72.

Coid J. (1993). Personality Disorder Reviewed Ed. by P. Tyrer and G. Stein, Gaskell, Royal College of Psychiatrists, London, 148.

Condon W.S. and Sander L.W. (1974). Neonate movement is synchronised with adult speech, Science 183, 99-101.

Damasio A. (1995). Descartes' Error, Emotion Reason and the Human Brain, Picador, London. 131-134, 100,102.

Edelman G. (1992). Bright Air Brilliant Fire, Penguin London, 227, 71.

Gunderson J. et al (1994). DSM-IV American Psychiatric Association, Diagnostic and Statistical Manual of Mental Disorders, Fourth Edition. Washington, D.C, American Psychiatric Association 1994, 629, 633.

Hall C. (1962). A Primer of Freudian Psychology, George Allen and Unwin Ltd, London, 72-119.

Holmes, T.H. and Rahe, R.H. (1967) The Social Readjustment Rating Scale. Journal of Psychosomatic Research, II, 213 – 218.

Jacobson B. and Bygdeman M. (1998). Obstetric care and proneness of offspring to suicide as adults: case-control study. BMJ, Volume 317, London, 1346 - 1349.
Kuhn T.S. (1962). The Structure of Scientific Revolutions. Chicago; University of Chicago Press.

Langs R. MD (1973). The techniques of Psychoanalytic Psychotherapy, Vol 1, Jason Aronson, Inc. New York, 243, 586.

Restak R.M. (1979). The Brain the Last Frontier, Warner Books Inc. New York, 200-202, 211.

Rose S. (1992). The Making of Memory, Bantam Press London, 218, 182, 158.

Salk I. Lipsitt L.P. Sturner W.Q. Reilly B.M. Levat R.H. Relationship of maternal and perinatal conditions to eventual adolescent suicide, Lancet, 1985;i:624-7.

Shalev A. Y. and Yehuda R. (1998), Psychological Trauma, American Psychiatric Press, Inc. 1400 Kay Street, N.W. Washington DC 20005, 39, 48, 32.

Sperry L. (1995). Handbook of Diagnosis and Treatment of the DSM IV Personality Disorders, Brunner/Mazel Inc. New York 6,7.

Sperry R. (1965). Brain bisection and the mechanisms of consciousness, in The Brain and Conscious Behaviour (Ed. J.C. Eccles) Springer, New York.

Springer S. and Deutsch D. (1981). Left Brain, Right Brain, W.H. Freeman and Company, San Fransisco, 172.

Stafford-Clark D. (1965). What Freud really said, McDonald & Co, Publishers Ltd, London, 120 -123, 55-59.

Thomas A. and Chess S. (1980). The dynamics of psychological development, Brunner Mazel, New York.

Tyrer P. Casey P. and Ferguson B. (1993). Personality Disorder Reviewed, Ed. by P. Tyrer and G. Stein, Gaskell, Royal College of Psychiatrists, London, 7, 12.

Werner E.E. & Smith R.S. (1982). Vulnerable but Invincible: a Study of Resilient Children. New York: McGraw-Hill.

Wilson S. (1993). Personality Disorder Reviewed, Ed. by P. Tyrer and G. Stein, Gaskell, Royal College of Psychiatrists, London, 187.

Wolberg L. (1982). The Practice of Psychotherapy, Brunner Mazel New York, 292, 45, 277.

Yehuda R. (1998), Psychological Trauma, American Psychiatric Press, Inc. 1400 Kay Street, N.W. Washington DC 20005, 98-100, 101.

Articles published:

1. Dec. 1976. "A Meditational Approach to Hypnosis and Autohypnosis". Proceedings of the British Society of Medical and Dental Hypnosis Vol. 2 No.3.

2. Dec. 1977. Complications, Risks and Dangers of Hypnosis with Children". Hypnos-nytt – the Swedish Journal of Clinical and Experimental Hypnosis, No. 6.

3. May 1978. "Hypnosis and the Neurological Model Part I". Hypnos – the Swedish Journal of Clinical and Experimental Hypnosis, No. 2.

4. Sept. 1978. "Hypnosis and the Neurological Model Part II". Hypnos – the Swedish Journal of Clinical and Experimental Hypnosis, No. 3-4.

5. Feb. 1979. "Hypnosis and the Neurological Model Part III". Hypnos – the Swedish Journal of Clinical and Experimental Hypnosis, No.1

6. Aug. 1979. "Hypnosis and the Neurological Model Part IV". Hypnos – the Swedish Journal of Clinical and Experimental Hypnosis, No.3-4.

7. Feb. 1984. Book Review "Hypnosis and Hypnotherapy with Children" by Gail Gardner and Karen Olness. Hypnos – the Swedish Journal of Hypnosis in Psychotherapy and Psychosomatic Medicine, Vol XI No.1.

8. May 1986. "N.L.P. – Fact or Fiction? Part I". Hypnos – The Swedish Journal of Hypnosis in Psychotherapy and Psychosomatic Medicine, Vol. XIII.

9. Sept. 1986. "N.L.P. – Fact or Fiction? Part II". Hypnos – The Swedish Journal of Hypnosis in Psychotherapy and Psychosomatic Medicine, Vol. XIII.

10. Dec. 1986. "N.L.P. – Fact or Fiction? Part III. Hypnos – The Swedish Journal of Hypnosis in Psychotherapy and Psychosomatic Medicine, Vol. XIII.

11. May 1988. "N.L.P." – An Alternative British Perspective". (A reply to an article by Dr. Michael Heap in the previous issue of Hypnos), Hypnos – The Swedish Journal of Hypnosis in Psychotherapy and Psychosomatic Medicine, Vol. XV.

12. June 1988. "Hypnosis with Children". Update – the Journal of Postgraduate General Practice. Vol. 36 No.11.

13. February 1992. "Traumatic Separation Theory" Hypnos, Swedish and European Journal of Hypnosis in Psychotherapy and Psychosomatic Medicine. Vol. XV1V No.1

14. August 1993. "Prenatal Transference" European Journal of Clinical Hypnosis Vol. No.1.

15. December 1993. "From Hypnoanalysis to Analytic Hypnotherapy – a Connecting Link" Hypnos – Swedish and European Journal of Hypnosis Vol. XX No.4.

16. August 1994 "Traumatic Separation Theory and Neurosis" Hypnotherapi – Journal of the Danish Medical Hypnosis Society Vol. No.3.

17. October 1995. “Change through Choices” Keynote address. Proceedings of First Africa Congress in Clinical Hypnosis and Psychosomatic Medicine, South Africa.

18. October 1995. “Traumatic Separation Theory, Hypnosis and Change” Proceedings of First Africa Congress in Clinical Hypnosis and Psychosomatic Medicine, South Africa.

20. June 1996. “20 Years of Teaching in Sweden”. Hypnos Nytt Svenska Foreningen for Klinisk & Experimental Hypnos. Sweden.

21. June 2002. “Traumatic Separation Theory and Personality Disorder” European Journal of Clinical Hypnosis, Volume 5 Issue 2.

22. June 2002. “NLP Facilitates Theory Therapy and Change in Personality Disorder: Traumatic Separation Theory” Rapport”, Issue No.s 56 and 58.

Comments from Colleagues

From: Maya Ulrich, Clinical Psychologist, Copenhagen University, Denmark - March 1991

On: Traumatic Separation Theory

"I have in the past year had the great pleasure to work with Don Ebrahim's theory and therapeutic interventions in my private practise as a clinical psychologist in Copenhagen.

My experience using Don Ebrahim's model of understanding the neurosis is best described by the following story.

Many years ago a man called Columbus decided, that he would try to reach India by sea setting out towards the west. He belonged to the group of people who found that the theory of the world being round made most sense, and therefore he now wanted to see India from a new angle.

When he returned he had found a new continent.

Important people at home envied Columbus for his discovery and popularity.

At a meeting with many important persons present they said to the guest of honour Mr Columbus: "What you did is in fact very easy - all of us could have done that".

Columbus stood up, took an egg from the table and replied: to find a new world is just as easy as being able to make this egg stand up.

They tried, in turn, to put the egg in an upright position. But all attempts failed. The egg kept rolling over onto its side.

Finally Columbus took the egg, gave it a little tap on the end - and it stood up.

The theory and therapy of Don Ebrahim is just as obvious, just as simple and just as genius as Columbus' egg.

What he has done is to gather useful knowledge from psychology and medicine across the established borders, mix it with common sense and 30 years of his own experimental experience and then with his eminent pedagogical capacity bring it about to all of us - and it makes sense.

I have in the past year presented the theory to many clients including torture victims from South Africa and the Middle-east, to psychology students (who I teach hypnosis to at the University of Copenhagen), to friends and relatives.

To most of them the theory makes sense.

And when I present the separation model in the first or second lesson with clients, many get better and their symptoms more tolerable just because of the deep insight and understanding they get about their problems and the relief of guilt which is a main point in the theoretical understanding. One of the first clients I showed the model to was a woman, whom I had been working with for one year using other methods. When I presented the model, tears silently rolled down her cheek, and she said: "I didn't know I was going to get a present today".

On another occasion I presented the theoretical model to a friend - an architect with no special knowledge of psychology - and he said “of course that is how it is” so quickly and naturally that I was quite astonished.

In comparison with my clinical work earlier I now work more cogently and therefore more quickly.

The single elements in Don Ebrahim's therapeutic method are well known as NLP and hypnoanalytical methods - but it is the context the INTEGRATION of it all which is so new and different. His sentence "Stop doing to yourself what your parents didn't do to you”, turns the most deeply rooted sentence in psychotherapy upside down and helps people to find an upright and vigorous position.

I am convinced that the book which Don Ebrahim is about to write, will make a revolution in psychotherapy."

From: Professor Herschel Prins, Midlands Centre for Criminology and Criminal Justice, University of Loughborough, UK, and Visiting Professor in Clinical Criminology, Nottingham Trent University UK - February 1997.

"Thanks very much for your paper which I have read with interest. Some of the ideas you have are very innovative and resonate for me, with the work of Winnicott - notably his work on the anti-social tendency".

From: Dr Brian Ferguson Consultant Psychiatrist Mapperley Hospital and Stonebridge Research Centre, Nottingham, England.

"I found it fascinating, both in the theoretical overview and the clinical material which you present. There is certainly much in it which is testable in a scientific manner and I would be very pleased to hear of any further studies you conduct looking at that issue" - February 1997.

From: Minette Bekker Clinical Psychologist P/Bag X 2023, Krugersdorp, 1740 South Africa - March 1997.

"I am a clinical psychologist at the Department of Correctional Services and am involved daily with traumatised persons. The workshop was of great value to me and I will be able to use the knowledge to good effect in my daily work."

From: Mavis Clark Educational Psychologist 12 Beech Road, Bedford View, 2008 South Africa - March 1997

"A privilege to be sponsored to attend the hypnosis workshop in Pretoria and I felt I gained a great deal of knowledge and insight. Thank you so much for making it possible."

From: Dr Frank J Vingoe Ph.D. Chartered Psychologist (Forensic and Clinical) Blackoak Road, Cyncoed, Cardiff , South Glamorgan - February 1997.

"...a creative and excellent paper". "Found it quite readable and full of interesting ideas".

From: Dr Michael Heap Ph.D. Centre for Psychotherapeutic Studies and President of the British Society of Experimental and Clinical Hypnosis - The University of Sheffield - March 1997.

"I have enjoyed reading it. It seems to me that separation, and the feeling and conflicts surrounding the experience, are potent sources of emotional distress and difficulty, and it is useful to have a theory which highlights its role in mental disorder and psychopathology".

From: Dr P E Gaarde-Madsen General Medical Practitioner and Hypnotherapist Vestre Alle 71, 9530 Stovring Denmark - January 1991.

"In about a half year I have been using your theory in practice, and I must congratulate you, your theories work like a miracle! The results were incredible. The clients changed very rapidly, they were deeply satisfied. I have now worked with about 5 to 10 clients in that way, the results as described. They were sent to me from a local youth-centre, where they have been for a long time using all their defences, bulimia and so on. They changed so rapidly and you can't recognise them".

From: Dr John E Barclay M.B. Ch.B., M.R.C. Psych., D.P.M. Consultant Psychiatrist - Retired, Rose Cottage, Fir Tree Lane Aughton, Lancs. October 1998.

"In his presentation of Traumatic Separation Theory Dr Ebrahim has distilled from the extensive field of Psychoanalytic theory what appears to be the commonest and most universal of mechanisms underlying personality pathology. He weaves a convincing and internally consistent and systematised theory; one which satisfyingly bridges both neurological and psychological models. I say "satisfying" since for a general and largely "organic" clinician the demonstration of physiological correlates is always more comfortable to live with.

In some measure the application of Dr Ebrahim's ideas is comparable to surgery; relatively little is required of the patient beyond a reasonably co-operative attitude. When combined with NLP it provides a framework for the active exposure of significant material as opposed to the passive and time-consuming waiting of more classic schools.

Taken together with the illustrative cases Dr Ebrahim's exposition promises an effective and excellently economic method for treatment. It is one by which the primarily non-dynamic clinician might more optimistically explore areas which he would have previously regarded with a noticeable lack of enthusiasm. It is an offering to tempt reconsideration of those cases which hitherto occupied the largely No-man's-land of clinical practice. It seems a significant and timely contribution to the literature".

Curriculum Vitae

Dr. Donald W. Ebrahim LRCP (Eng.) MRCS (Lond.)

After qualifying from Sheffield University Medical School in 1952, he held hospital posts in Paediatrics and Orthopaedics. A brief spell of service in the Royal Army Medical Corps was followed by general practice in Coventry.

As a single handed G.P. for twenty five years, he used hypnosis for a wide variety of problems. He was also in charge of a school for emotionally disturbed children during this time, developing innovatory techniques in group hypnosis settings.

Since 1971 he has lectured for the British Society of Medical and Dental Hypnosis. In 1976 the Swedish Society for Experimental and Clinical Hypnosis invited him to demonstrate his techniques with children. Ever since, his workshops and lectures have formed part of their three-year training programme in hypnosis for psychiatrists and psychologists.

In 1981 the B.B.C. invited him to take part in their television documentary "Hypnosis and Healing" and again in 1984 in "Alternative Medicine".

In June 1982 he completed 350 hours training in short-term Psychoanalytic psychotherapy under the personal supervision of Prof. Lewis Wolberg M.D. and Prof. Arlene Wolberg Ph. D. of the Postgraduate Centre for Mental Health, University of New York. Since then he has been in full-time private practice in psychotherapy.

He was co-chairperson with Gordon Ambrose, Gail Gardner and Karen Olness in the Paediatric workshop at the 9th International Congress in Hypnosis and Psychosomatic Medicine held in Glasgow in 1983, and was workshop chairperson at the 2nd, 3rd, and the 6th European congresses in subsequent years.

In 1986 he was invited to be the keynote speaker on hypnosis at the Canada West Medical Congress, and in the same year he obtained a Master Practitioner's Certificate in Neurolinguistic Programming (NLP). Since then he has been conducting NLP seminars in Scandinavia and the U.K. with particular emphasis on its application in psychotherapy and education.

He has published several articles on hypnosis, its neurological aspects and clinical applications; and NLP. In 1988 he evolved a new model of

Personality Disorder – Traumatic Separation Theory and has been teaching its application in short-term dynamic psychotherapy, in Sweden, Denmark and South Africa.

On 23 September 1994 in Gotenburg Sweden, he was awarded The Annie Fasth Foundation Prize for his development of Traumatic Separation Theory and researching its clinical applications.

He is a member of the British Society of Experimental and Clinical Hypnosis; and has been awarded honorary memberships of the Swedish Society of Experimental and Clinical Hypnosis, and the Danish Society of Medical Hypnosis in recognition of his teaching. And the South African Society of Clinical Hypnosis has presented him with their Certificate of Tribute.